Know Your
Bible
for Kids
All About Jesus

Donna K. Maltese
Illustrated by David Miles

BARBOUR BOOKS
An Imprint of Barbour Publishing, Inc.

Our mission is to publish and distribute inspirational products offering exceptional value and biblical encouragement to the masses.

 Member of the
Evangelical Christian
Publishers Association

Introduction

Jesus is a mysterious, captivating, and awesome person. His story is told from the first to the last page of the Bible. He wants you to know who He was, has been, and always will be—the one who gave His life to save yours so that you could be a part of God's amazing plan.

In this fascinating book, *Know Your Bible for Kids—All About Jesus*, we have chosen 100 of the most interesting things about Jesus, the King of kings and Lord of lords. Every illuminating entry follows this outline:

- *Who, where, or what is this person, place, or thing?*
  A brief description of a character, site, or term.
- *What's it all about?*
  Details about the background of this character, site, or term as it relates to Jesus.
- *What's an important verse about that person, place, or thing?*
  A key Bible verse about that character, site, or term.
- *What does that mean to me?*
  What that character, site, or term teaches God's followers about Jesus.

One of the awesome things about Jesus is that He has always been with us, from Genesis to Revelation. He is our timeless Rock and Refuge. Within this book, you will rediscover Jesus from A to Z, beginning with the description of Him as the "Alpha and Omega" and concluding with His never-ending reign in "Zion," the heavenly Jerusalem.

You'll learn more and more insights into His nature and His immense love for us all as He comes to life on every page. We invite you to use this fun, fascinating, and fact-filled book to better understand God's plan, His provision of the Spirit, His love for His one and only Son, Jesus, and how, in following Him, you'll find the depth and breadth of Christ in your walk and way every day!

Alpha and Omega

What is the Alpha and Omega?

Alpha and *Omega* are Greek words. In English, *Alpha* means "first" and *Omega* means "last."

What's it all about?

A man named John had a revelation or vision. In it, he heard Jesus call Himself "the Alpha and the Omega."

What's an important verse about the Alpha and Omega?

[A voice] said, "(I am the First and the Last.) Write in a book what you see and send it to the seven churches."
REVELATION 1:11 NLV

What does that mean to me?

God wants you and everyone else to get His message: Jesus is all powerful. He has been and always will be here, helping you—and everyone else—from the beginning to the end. Jesus is all you will ever need.

Andrew

Who is Andrew?

A fisherman, one of Jesus' main disciples (followers), and a brother of Simon Peter from the town of Bethsaida.

What's it all about?

One day, over 5,000 hungry people came to Jesus. Andrew told Jesus what food they had on hand, but he couldn't see it going very far. Yet after Jesus thanked God for the food, there was enough for everyone—plus leftovers!

What's an important verse about Andrew?

Andrew. . .said, "Here is a boy with five small loaves of barley bread. He also has two small fish. But how far will that go in such a large crowd?"
JOHN 6:8–9 NIrV

What does that mean to me?

Thank God for what you have, and Jesus will grow it into more than you can imagine!

Angels

What are angels?

Heavenly creatures. God sends some out to deliver messages to people. Some guard or take care of people. Others worship God in heaven.

What's it all about?

The angel Gabriel announced the coming of John the Baptist and Jesus. Others warned Jesus' foster father, Joseph, of danger. Angels were with Jesus for His birth, life, death, resurrection (rising from the grave), and ascension (going back to heaven).

What's an important verse about angels?

Are not all the angels spirits who work for God? They are sent out to help those who are to be saved from the punishment of sin.
HEBREWS 1:14 NLV

What does that mean to me?

Angels were always looking out for Jesus and His followers, and they are certainly looking out for you, too. Though you may not be able to see them, never fear! Your angels are near!

Ascension

What is the ascension?

When Jesus went up (ascended) to heaven after His resurrection (rising from the dead).

What's it all about?

After ascending to be with Father God, Jesus sent the Holy Spirit to take care of us—just like Jesus promised.

What's an important verse about the ascension?

As they strained to see him rising into heaven, two white-robed men suddenly stood among them. "Men of Galilee," they said. . ."Jesus has been taken from you into heaven, but someday he will return from heaven in the same way you saw him go!"
ACTS 1:10–11 NLT

What does that mean to me?

Rest easy. Jesus will be back someday. Meanwhile, the Holy Spirit will guide you and fill you with power!

Author of Faith

Who is the Author of Faith?

Jesus is!

What's it all about?

The life and death of Jesus is an amazing tale that tells us how we can get close to God again. And Jesus is the *author* of that story! By His life, He has shown us how to live right. All we need to do is keep looking to Him for guidance and following the words in His Book. He'll make our way perfect!

What's an important verse about the Author of Faith?

Let us keep on running the race marked out for us. Let us keep looking to Jesus. He is the one who started this journey of faith. And he is the one who completes the journey of fath. . . . So think about him. Then you won't get tired. You won't lose hope.
HEBREWS 12:1–3 NIrV

What does that mean to me?

God has given you everything you need to live a wonderful life with Him. Just keep your eyes and mind on Jesus—and the Author will write you a happy ending!

Baptism

What is baptism?

A Christian ceremony where people who believe in Jesus are dipped in or sprinkled with water.

What's it all about?

John the Baptist baptized lots of people. When he baptized Jesus, heaven opened and God's Spirit, which looked like a dove, landed on Jesus. Then a voice from heaven said, "This is my son who I love." In the early days of the Christian church, believers young and old were baptized.

What's an important verse about baptism?

This baptism has nothing to do with removing dirt from your body. Instead, it promises God that you will keep a clear sense of right and wrong.
1 PETER 3:21 NIrV

What does that mean to me?

When you are baptized, it symbolizes your faith in God. Your heart is one with the heart of Jesus, and the Holy Spirit will help you understand what is right and wrong in God's eyes.

Barabbas

Who is Barabbas?

A murderer who was in prison.

What's it all about?

After being arrested, Jesus was brought to Pilate, a Roman governor. But Pilate found Jesus had done nothing wrong. So he offered to set either Barabbas or Jesus free. The crowd chose Barabbas.

What's an important verse about Barabbas?

"Which one of the two do you want me to let go free?" They said, "Barabbas". . . . Pilate let Barabbas go free but he had men whip Jesus. Then he handed Him over to be nailed to a cross.
MATTHEW 27:21, 26 NLV

What does that mean to me?

Jesus died so that even the worst of sinners could be set free. No matter what you have done, Jesus can save you!

Bartimaeus

Who is Bartimaeus?

A blind man sitting along the roadside in Jericho when Jesus walked by.

What's it all about?

Bartimaeus kept yelling for Jesus to have pity on him, even when other people told him to be quiet. When Jesus told His disciples to call the blind man, Bartimaeus took off his coat and ran to Jesus.

What's an important verse about Bartimaeus?

The blind man said to Him, "Lord, I want to see!" Jesus said, "Go! Your faith has healed you." At once he could see and he followed Jesus down the road.
MARK 10:51–52 NLV

What does that mean to me?

Need help? Yell out to Jesus. Then, when He calls you, leave everything behind and run to Him. He'll open your eyes of faith!

Bethany

What is Bethany?

A town about a mile and a half from Jerusalem, Israel.

What's it all about?

Bethany is where Lazarus lived with his sisters, Mary and Martha. It's also where a woman poured expensive perfume on Jesus' feet.

What's an important verse about Bethany?

Jesus led his disciples out to the area near Bethany. Then he lifted up his hands and blessed them. While he was blessing them, he left them. He was taken up into heaven. Then they worshiped him. With great joy, they returned to Jerusalem.
LUKE 24:50–52 NIrV

What does that mean to me?

The love and blessings of Jesus keep coming, even though He is now in heaven. That's news that can make you happy—even on the saddest of days!

Bethlehem

What is Bethlehem?

A town five miles from Jerusalem, Israel. Also called Zion and the City of David, Bethlehem is where Jesus was born.

What's it all about?

Many years ago, God spoke to a prophet named Micah, telling him that someday a ruler would be born in Bethlehem. This ruler would be a shepherd for God's people.

What's an important verse about Bethlehem?

"Today in the town of David a Savior has been born to you. He is the Messiah the Lord. Here is how you will know I am telling you the truth. You will find a baby wrapped in strips of cloth and lying in a manger." LUKE 2:11–12 NIrV

What does that mean to me?

You can always trust God. He always keeps His promises—He brought a Savior among us!

Bible

What is the Bible?

A book containing 66 smaller books, each written by prophets inspired by God.

What's it all about?

The Bible has two parts. The first is the Old Testament, which is sometimes called the scriptures or holy book. That has 39 books and was written before Jesus was born. The second part is the New Testament. That has 27 books and was written about Jesus after He ascended to heaven.

What's an important verse about the Bible?

God has breathed life into all Scripture. It is useful for teaching us what is true. It is useful for correcting our mistakes. It is useful for making our lives whole again. It is useful for training us to do what is right. By using Scripture, the servant of God can be completely prepared to do every good thing.
2 TIMOTHY 3:16–17 NIrV

What does that mean to me?

You can trust the Bible to guide you in all things. You can't go wrong by following what God has written!

Bridegroom

What is a bridegroom?

A person who loves and marries his wife.

What's it all about?

Jesus is the Bridegroom to the Church—all believers everywhere! He loved us so much that He died on the cross to save us. Now He wants those who follow Him to be one with Him, like a wife is with a husband.

What's an important verse about a bridegroom?

Scriptures say, "A man leaves his father and mother and is joined to his wife, and the two are united into one." This is a great mystery, but it is an illustration of the way Christ and the church are one.
EPHESIANS 5:31–32 NLT

What does that mean to me?

Spend time with Jesus. The more you do, the better you'll know and love Him.

Caiaphas, the High Priest

Who is Caiaphas, the High Priest?

He was the top leader of the Jews the year Jesus was crucified.

What's it all about?

After His arrest, Jesus was taken to Caiaphas and put on trial. But Caiaphas had already decided that Jesus should be killed—which, it turns out, was part of God's plan.

What's an important verse about Caiaphas, the High Priest?

Caiaphas was the one who had told the other Jewish leaders, "It's better that one man should die for the people." JOHN 18:14 NLT

What does that mean to me?

Leave everything in God's hands—the good and the bad—because He can use anything, anyone, and any situation to make His plans come true!

Commission to the Disciples

What is the commission to the disciples?

The job Jesus gave His disciples to do.

What's it all about?

After Jesus died and rose again, He gave His followers an order: to go all over the world and spread the word about Him.

What's an important verse about the commission to the disciples?

Jesus came to them. He said. . ."Go and make disciples of

all nations. Baptize them in the name of the Father and of the Son and of the Holy Spirit. Teach them to obey everything I have commanded you. And you can be sure that I am always with you, to the very end."
MATTHEW 28:18–20 NIrV

What does that mean to me?

All believers—then and now, you and me—are to spread the word about Jesus and teach people to love God and each other. He has promised to never, ever leave us as we carry out His mission!

Controls Nature

Who controls nature?

Jesus. He can stop the wind and calm the waves.

What's it all about?

Jesus and His disciples decided to cross a lake in a boat.
While they were on the water, a big storm came up.
The waves were very high, and the boat began filling
with water. Jesus was asleep at the back of the boat. His
followers got scared, began shouting, and woke Him up.

What's an important verse about controlling nature?

When Jesus woke up, he rebuked the wind and said to the waves, "Silence! Be still!" Suddenly the wind stopped, and there was a great calm. Then he asked them, "Why are you afraid? Do you still have no faith?"
MARK 4:39–40 NLT

What does that mean to me?

When storms come into your life, trust in Jesus. He's already in your boat. So don't be scared. He's in control. Have faith that He will make everything turn out all right.

Cornerstone

What is a cornerstone?

A cornerstone is a big solid rock. It is on that rock, the foundation, that people build. If this rock is removed, the whole building might crash down!

What's it all about?

Jesus is our cornerstone. He's the solid rock, the sure foundation, on which the Christian Church was built and on which we stand.

What's an important verse about a cornerstone?

You belong in God's family. This family is built on the teachings of the missionaries and the early preachers. Jesus Christ Himself is the cornerstone, which is the most important part of the building. Christ keeps this building together and it is growing into a holy building for the Lord. You are also being put together as a part of this building because God lives in you by His Spirit.
EPHESIANS 2:19–22 NLV

With Jesus as your cornerstone, you can stand up against anything—because God lives in you and you are part of His family!

Creator

Who is the Creator?

Jesus is! That's why He is so powerful!

What's it all about?

Jesus not only made everything we see; He made everything we *don't* see! And not only is He our awesome Creator, but He's our Sustainer, too. That means He keeps everything going. He made each of us and keeps us all breathing. He keeps the clouds up in the sky and the planets in the heavens.

What's an important verse about the Creator?

Christ made everything in the heavens and on the earth. He made everything that is seen and things that are not seen. He made all the powers of heaven. Everything was made by Him and for Him. Christ was before all things. All things are held together by Him.
COLOSSIANS 1:16–17 NLV

What does that mean to me?

Because Jesus is the Creator, He can help *you* with your own creations. Tap into His power. He'll make your ideas even better!

Cross

What is a cross?

A long piece of wood that has a shorter piece across it, close to the top.

What's it all about?

The Roman government punished people by nailing them to a wooden cross. The long end of the cross would be stuck in the ground, and people would hang there until they died.

What's an important verse about a cross?

We know that our old life, our old sinful self, was nailed to the cross with Christ. And so the power of sin that held us was destroyed. Sin is no longer our boss.
Romans 6:6 nlv

What does that mean to me?

If you believe in Jesus, you are free from sin's power! Instead, you are filled with God's power. *He's* the one who brought Jesus back to life.

Crucifixion

What is the crucifixion?

When Jesus was nailed to the cross to pay for our sins (wrongdoings).

What's it all about?

Jesus hadn't done anything wrong, but the religious leaders didn't like Him. So they got the Roman governor to crucify Jesus on the cross. It was all part of God's plan to bring us back to Him.

What's an important verse about the Crucifixion?

I have been crucified with Christ. I don't live any longer, but Christ lives in me. . . . He loved me and gave himself for me.
GALATIANS 2:20 NIrV

What does that mean to me?

God took the part of you that has trouble following rules and put it on the cross with Jesus Christ. When Jesus was buried, your sins were buried, too—forever!

Denial of Peter

What is the denial of Peter?

Jesus knew a follower named Peter would one day tell people he didn't know Jesus.

What's it all about?

When Jesus was arrested, Peter got scared. Three times he denied knowing Him!

What's an important verse about the denial of Peter?

Peter remembered what Jesus had said. "The rooster will crow," Jesus had told him. "Before it does, you will say three times that you don't know me." Peter went outside. He broke down and cried.
MATTHEW 26:75 NIrV

What does that mean to me?

Sooner or later, you may be sorry for the things you have done. When that happens, remember that Jesus, who knows all, has already forgiven you. And can still use you!

Devil

What is the devil?

A very bad (evil) spiritual being.

What's it all about?

Jesus called the devil the father of lies. He was the serpent in the Garden of Eden who talked Eve into disobeying God. And he has been tricking people ever since!

What's an important verse about the devil?

Dear children, don't let anyone lead you astray. . . . The person who does what is sinful belongs to the devil. That's because the devil has been sinning from the beginning. But the Son of God came to destroy the devil's work.

1 JOHN 3:7–8 NIrV

What does that mean to me?

If you obey God and follow Jesus, the devil will lose his influence over you!

Disciples

What are disciples?

People who follow the teachings of Jesus.

What's it all about?

Jesus had 12 main disciples: Simon Peter and his brother
Andrew; James, son of Zebedee, and his brother John;
Philip and Bartholomew; Thomas; Matthew, the tax
collector; James, son of Alphaeus; Thaddaeus; Simon, the
Zealot; and Judas Iscariot.

What's an important verse about disciples?

Jesus called together the 12 disciples. He gave them
power and authority to drive out all demons and to heal
sicknesses. Then he sent them out to announce God's
kingdom and to heal those who were sick.
LUKE 9:1–2 NIrV

What does that mean to me?

When you answer Jesus' calling and make Him first
in your life, you, too, can be His disciple. That's some
powerful stuff!

Foot Washing

What is foot washing?

When you wash your own feet or someone else's.

What's it all about?

The night before His arrest, Jesus was at dinner with His 12 disciples. Before eating, Jesus wrapped a towel around Himself, poured water into a bowl, and washed and dried all His disciples' feet.

What's an important verse about foot washing?

"Since I, your Lord and Teacher, have washed your feet, you ought to wash each other's feet. I have given you an example to follow. Do as I have done to you. I tell you the truth, slaves are not greater than their master."
JOHN 13:14–16 NLT

What does that mean to me?

True happiness comes from doing something for someone else. Who can you "do for" today?

Gabriel

Who is Gabriel?

An angel or messenger of God.

What's it all about?

In the Old Testament, Gabriel talked with Daniel. In the New Testament, God sent Gabriel to tell Zacharias he would have a son. Then God sent Gabriel with an important message for Mary.

What's an important verse about Gabriel?

Gabriel appeared to her and said, "Greetings, favored woman! The Lord is with you!" Confused and disturbed, Mary tried to think what the angel could mean. "Don't be afraid, Mary," the angel told her, "for you have found favor with God! You will conceive and give birth to a son, and you will name him Jesus."
LUKE 1:28–31 NLT

What does that mean to me?

Puzzled? Don't worry. When God sends you a message, He'll make sure it's clear!

Galilee

What is Galilee?

A region in northern Israel.

What's it all about?

Jesus spent His childhood in Nazareth, a town in Galilee. Eleven of Jesus' 12 disciples (all but Judas Iscariot) and most of the women who followed Jesus came from Galilee. At a wedding in Cana, a town in Galilee, they ran out of wine. So Jesus turned water into wine.

What's an important verse about Galilee?

What Jesus did here in Cana in Galilee was the first of his signs. Jesus showed his glory by doing this sign. And his disciples believed in him.
JOHN 2:11 NIrV

What does that mean to me?

Jesus is so powerful that He can work miracles whenever and wherever you are. That's a faith booster!

Gethsemane

Where is Gethsemane?

This olive grove is a little way up the Mount of Olives in Jerusalem, Israel.

What's it all about?

Jesus took all but one of His disciples with Him to Gethsemane. He kept three of them even closer. In Gethsemane, Jesus prayed so hard that He sweat drops of blood. Later a mob, led by Judas Iscariot, came to arrest Him.

What's an important verse about Gethsemane?

Jesus went with them to the olive grove called Gethsemane, and he said, "Sit here while I go over there to pray." He took Peter and Zebedee's two sons, James and John, and he became anguished and distressed. . . . He went on a little farther and bowed with his face to the ground, praying.

MATTHEW 26:36–37, 39 NLT

What does that mean to me?

Get closer to Jesus when you are upset or hurt. He can help you because He knows just what you are going through.

Golden Rule

What is the Golden Rule?

That we should only interact with others in ways that we would like others to act toward us.

What's it all about?

Jesus told us not only how to follow God, but also how to live with other people. We are to treat them as we would have them treat us. If everyone would do that, peace, love, and understanding would rule!

What's an important verse about the Golden Rule?

"Do for other people whatever you would like to have them do for you. This is what the Jewish Law and the early preachers said."
MATTHEW 7:12 NLV

What does that mean to me?

Be good to other people—no matter how they treat you. That Golden Rule rules!

Golgotha

Where is Golgotha?

In Jesus' day, Golgotha was just outside of Jerusalem. Today, Golgotha is inside Jerusalem's walls.

What's it all about?

The Hebrew word *Golgotha* and the Latin word *Calvary* both mean "the skull." It's where Romans crucified criminals.

What's an important verse about Golgotha?

They brought Jesus to a place called Golgotha (which means "Place of the Skull"). They offered him wine drugged with myrrh, but he refused it. Then the soldiers nailed him to the cross.
MARK 15:22–24 NLT

What does that mean to me?

After suffering at Golgotha, Jesus died—but then He came back to life, and He still lives today! So no matter how bad things look, don't worry or be scared. God will make good out of it!

Good Shepherd

Who is the Good Shepherd?

Jesus Christ is!

What's it all about?

Jesus is our shepherd—and we are the sheep He takes care of. He talks to our hearts so that we will know His voice and be sure to follow Him. Jesus will always protect us and watch over us. He will never leave us, and He will always give us what we need.

What's an important verse about the Good Shepherd?

"I am the Good Shepherd. The Good Shepherd gives His life for the sheep. . . . I know My sheep and My sheep know Me."
JOHN 10:11, 14 NLV

What does that mean to me?

Jesus laid down His life so you could live forever. So stick close to Him. His mission is to take good care of you. Your mission? Get to know Him better by reading your Bible. Learn all you can about Him. He already knows everything about you.

Gospels–Matthew, Mark, Luke, John

What are the Gospels?

The books in the Bible that tell the life, death, and resurrection stories of Jesus.

What's it all about?

Matthew, Mark, Luke, and John each wrote a story all about Jesus and His life. These stories, or *gospels*, are the first four books of the New Testament in the Bible. Matthew wrote his story for Jews. Mark wrote for Romans. Luke wrote for non-Jews. And John wrote for all believers. The word *gospel* means "good news." Because that's what Jesus is!

What's an important verse about the Gospels?

I. . .decided to write down an orderly report of exactly what happened. I am doing this for you, most excellent Theophilus. I want you to know that the things you have been taught are true.
LUKE 1:3–4 NIrv

The gospel stories are exact accounts of Jesus' life. So read and believe them. They are packed full of good news for you and me!

Greatest Commandments

What are the greatest commandments?

The two most important rules Jesus wants us to follow.

What's it all about?

God gave Moses lots of laws His people were to obey. When Jesus came along, He said that His law of love would take care of all other laws.

What's an important verse about the greatest commandments?

Jesus replied, " 'You must love the LORD your God with all your heart, all your soul, and all your mind.' This is the first and greatest commandment. A second is equally important: 'Love your neighbor as yourself.' "
MATTHEW 22:37–39 NLT

What does that mean to me?

If you truly love God, yourself, and others with all that you are, you will make God, yourself, and the rest of the world happy.

Heaven

What is heaven?

A place beyond the clouds.

What's it all about?

Heaven is where God and Jesus are now. It's also where the souls and spirits of Christians go after their bodies die.

What's an important verse about heaven?

"Love your enemies! Do good to them. Lend to them without expecting to be repaid. Then your reward from heaven will be very great, and you will truly be acting as children of the Most High."
LUKE 6:35 NLT

What does that mean to me?

The more you act like God here on earth, the more you will be rewarded for it in heaven—and the more you'll make your world like a little piece of heaven on earth!

Herod the Great

Who is Herod the Great?

A king of Judea who was part Jewish and part Roman.

What's it all about?

When Herod heard the "king of the Jews" (Jesus) had been born, Herod got jealous. In his eyes, there was no room for another king. So he sent soldiers to kill baby Jesus. But an angel warned Jesus' foster father, Joseph, in a dream. They escaped!

What's an important verse about Herod the Great?

After Herod died, Joseph had a dream. . . . The angel said, "Get up! Take the child and his mother. Go to the land of Israel. The people who were trying to kill the child are dead."
MATTHEW 2:19–20 NIrV

What does that mean to me?

Keep your ears open to God's messengers. They'll keep you safe!

Hidden Manna

What is hidden manna?

Manna is the stuff God rained down from heaven to feed the Israelites in the wilderness after they fled Egypt. Jesus is the "hidden manna."

What's it all about?

God gives us everything we need to eat, live, love, smile, and breathe. And the best thing He has blessed us with is Jesus. He is our "top-secret provision"—all we ever really need comes from and is found in Him.

What's an important verse about hidden manna?

"Anyone with ears to hear must listen to the Spirit and understand what he is saying to the churches. To everyone who is victorious I will give some of the manna that has been hidden away in heaven."
REVELATION 2:17 NLT

What does that mean to me?

You can depend on Jesus to supply *everything* you need!

Holy Spirit

Who is the Holy Spirit?

God's spiritual presence living within Jesus' followers, sent to comfort, inspire, and help.

What's it all about?

When Jesus went back to heaven, He sent believers the Holy Spirit to guide them, teach them, and be their friend.

What's an important verse about the Holy Spirit?

All the believers gathered in one place. Suddenly a sound came from heaven. It was like a strong wind blowing. It filled the whole house where they were sitting. . . . All of them were filled with the Holy Spirit.
ACTS 2:1–2, 4 NIrV

What does that mean to me?

When you became a believer, the Holy Spirit came to live inside you. So you have a very close friend. Ask Him to teach and guide you!

I Am

Who is the I Am?

God *and* Jesus.

What's it all about?

When Moses asked God what His name was, He said He was the "I Am." Later, Jesus said that He, too, was the I Am. That means God and Jesus always have been, always are, and always will be. Jesus also said He is the Bread of Life; Light of the world; Door; Good Shepherd; Resurrection and Life; the Way, the Truth, and the Life; and true Vine!

What's an important verse about the I Am?

"How can you say you have seen Abraham?" Jesus answered, "I tell you the truth, before Abraham was even born, I AM!"
JOHN 8:57–58 NLT

What does that mean to me?

Jesus was, is, and always will be whatever you need, wherever and whenever you need Him!

James, Son of Zebedee

Who is James, son of Zebedee?

One of Jesus' main disciples and a brother of John.

What's it all about?

James was a fisherman working with his brother John, his father Zebedee, and his friend Simon Peter. As soon as Jesus called James, he left his boat and father and went with Jesus. James, John, and Peter were very close to Jesus.

What's an important verse about James, son of Zebedee?

King Herod arrested some people who belonged to the church. He planned to make them suffer greatly. He had James killed with a sword. James was John's brother.
ACTS 12:1–2 NIrV

What does that mean to me?

James loved Jesus so much that he was willing to die for Him. Does Jesus mean that much to you?

Jerusalem

Where is Jerusalem?

Also called the City of David and Zion, Jerusalem is in Israel.

What's it all about?

Jerusalem is where the temple was built. When Jesus was born, His parents took Him to the Jerusalem Temple to dedicate Him to God. Later, outside of Jerusalem's walls, Jesus was killed.

What's an important verse about Jerusalem?

Jesus began to explain to his disciples what would happen to him. He told them he must go to Jerusalem. There he. . . must be killed and on the third day rise to life again.
MATTHEW 16:21 NIrV

What does that mean to me?

Jesus knows everything that has happened, is happening, and will happen—even in your life! So don't worry. He's got everything figured out, and it's all good.

John the Baptist

Who is John the Baptist?

The cousin of Jesus.

What's it all about?

An angel told Zachariah that he would have a son in his old age. Nine months later, his son, John the Baptist, was born. John lived in the wilderness and ate honey and locusts. Later, he baptized Jesus in the Jordan River.

What's an important verse about John the Baptist?

"You yourselves are witnesses that I said, 'I am not the Messiah. I was sent ahead of him'. . . . He must become more important. I must become less important."
JOHN 3:28, 30 NIrv

What does that mean to me?

You are very important to Jesus. Are you willing to make Him the *most* important thing in your life?

John, Son of Zebedee

Who is John, son of Zebedee?

One of Jesus' main disciples and the brother of James.

What's it all about?

John fished with James, Zebedee, and Simon Peter. When Jesus called, John dropped the net he was mending and followed Jesus! This disciple wrote the Bible books of John and Revelation.

What's an important verse about John, son of Zebedee?

When Jesus saw his mother standing there beside the disciple he loved, he said to her, "Dear woman, here is your son." And he said to this disciple, "Here is your mother." And from then on this disciple took her into his home.
JOHN 19:26–27 NLT

What does that mean to me?

Jesus trusted John with His mother. Is Jesus trusting you with someone or something?

Joseph, Foster Father of Jesus

Who is Joseph, foster father of Jesus?

A good man, carpenter, descendant of David, and husband to Mary.

What's it all about?

Joseph planned to marry Mary. But he changed his mind when he found out she was pregnant—until God's angel came to him in a dream.

What's an important verse about Joseph, foster father of Jesus?

The angel said, "Joseph, son of David, don't be afraid to take Mary home as your wife. The baby inside her is from the Holy Spirit. She is going to have a son. You must give him the name Jesus."
MATTHEW 1:20–21 NIrV

What does that mean to me?

Be like Joseph: keep your ears open to hear God's good plan for your life—and follow it!

Joseph of Arimathea

Who is Joseph of Arimathea?

A rich man from Arimathea.

What's it all about?

Joseph, a leader in the Jewish Council, didn't agree with the council's decision to kill Jesus. That's because Joseph was a follower of Jesus in secret. He didn't want others to know because he was afraid. Later, Joseph buried Jesus in his own tomb.

What's an important verse about Joseph of Arimathea?

Joseph went boldly to Pilate and asked for Jesus' body. . . . He took down the body and wrapped it in the linen. He put it in a tomb cut out of rock. Then he rolled a stone against the entrance.

MARK 15:43, 46 NIrV

What does that mean to me?

God will give you courage—just when you need it!

Judas Iscariot

Who is Judas Iscariot?

One of Jesus' main disciples *and* the one who betrayed Him.

What's it all about?

Judas didn't like some of the ways Jesus did things. So, for 30 pieces of silver, he handed Jesus over to His enemies, who then killed Him. Later, Judas hung himself.

What's an important verse about Judas Iscariot?

Judas was sorry he had handed Jesus over when he saw that Jesus was going to be killed. He took back the thirty

pieces of silver and gave it to the head religious leaders and the other leaders. He said, "I have sinned because I handed over a Man Who has done no wrong." And they said, "What is that to us? That is your own doing."
MATTHEW 27:3–4 NLV

What does that mean to me?

Stay on the right and faithful path by loving God and Jesus much more than money.

Kingdom of Heaven (or God)

What is the kingdom of heaven (or God)?

The peace believers feel inside their spirits and hearts. It's also where believers will live after Jesus comes back.

What's it all about?

When we totally count on God to take care of everything in our lives, we are living in the kingdom of heaven!

What's an important verse about the kingdom of heaven (or God)?

Jesus said, "What I'm about to tell you is true. You need to change and become like little children. If you don't, you will never enter the kingdom of heaven."
MATTHEW 18:3 NIrV

What does that mean to me?

No matter how things look, put *all* your trust in God. You'll find yourself in His royal palace—where He alone is King!

Lamb of God

Who is the Lamb of God?

Jesus is!

What's it all about?

In Old Testament days, God's people would kill (sacrifice) a perfect lamb. The blood of that lamb cleansed people of their sins so that they could get close to God. When Jesus died on the cross, He became *our* perfect Lamb!

What's an important verse about the Lamb of God?

The next day John the Baptist saw Jesus coming to him. He said, "See! The Lamb of God Who takes away the sin of the world!"
JOHN 1:29 NLV

What does that mean to me?

Jesus shed His blood to save you from your sins. Because of Him, you can snuggle up close to God! Thank Jesus for His sacrifice today.

Last Supper

What is the Last Supper?

The last meal Jesus ate with His followers before He was killed.

What's it all about?

Hours before His arrest, Jesus and His 12 main disciples had a Passover meal in Jerusalem where Jesus washed his followers' feet. Then He told them to break bread and drink wine in memory of that night and God's new promise—that all who believe in Jesus will be saved.

What's an important verse about the Last Supper?

Jesus took bread. He gave thanks and broke it. He handed it to them [His followers] and said, "This is my body. It is given for you". . . . In the same way, after the supper he took the cup. He said, "This cup is the new covenant in my blood. It is poured out for you."
LUKE 22:19–20 NIrV

What does that mean to me?

Remember Jesus always. Know that He is all you need to be saved!

Lazarus

Who is Lazarus?

A brother of Mary and Martha of Bethany.

What's it all about?

Jesus loved His friend Lazarus so much that He cried when Lazarus died. Then Jesus brought His friend back to life!

What's an important verse about Lazarus?

Jesus loved Martha and her sister and Lazarus. But when He heard that Lazarus was sick, He stayed where He was two more days. . . . Then Jesus said to [His followers], "Lazarus is dead. Because of you I am glad I was not there so that you may believe. Come, let us go to him."
JOHN 11:5–6, 14–15 NLV

What does that mean to me?

Never give up hope. Jesus *will* come to help you! In His own time and all to God's glory!

Light of the World

Who is the Light of the world?

Jesus is!

What's it all about?

Jesus is not only our Savior, but He is also light! When He shines His light, we can see more clearly what is right and wrong.

What's an important verse about the Light of the world?

Jesus spoke to the people again. He said, "I am the light of the world. Anyone who follows me will never walk in darkness. They will have that light. They will have life." JOHN 8:12 NIrV

What does that mean to me?

Your path is clear and your steps sure when you walk in the Light! So follow Jesus closely. He'll keep the darkness away—and help your own light to shine.

Lion of the Tribe of Judah

Who is the Lion of the tribe of Judah?

Jesus is!

What's it all about?

The name *Judah* means "to praise." Jesus, from the Jewish tribe of Judah, burst out of the grave like a lion, and all His enemies scattered! Nothing can keep Him down or hold Him back. He wins every battle.

What's an important verse about the Lion of the tribe of Judah?

"Stop weeping! Look, the Lion of the tribe of Judah, the heir to David's throne, has won the victory. He is worthy to open the scroll and its seven seals."
REVELATION 5:5 NLT

What does that mean to me?

If you have a problem, praise Jesus—your foes will flee and your load will lighten!

Living Water

What is living water?

The Spirit that enters believers in Jesus.

What's it all about?

When you let Jesus into your heart, He sends the Holy Spirit to live inside you. That Spirit is like living water. It cools down and peps up all who are thirsty for God and for doing right.

What's an important verse about living water?

Jesus stood up and spoke in a loud voice. He said, "Let anyone who is thirsty come to me and drink. Does anyone believe in me? Then, just as Scripture says, rivers of living water will flow from inside them."
JOHN 7:37–38 NIrV

What does that mean to me?

Drink in Jesus and watch your doubts and fears get flushed out!

Loaves and Fishes

What are the loaves and fishes?

The miracle of the loaves and fishes is the only one that appears in all four Gospels—Matthew, Mark, Luke, and John.

What's it all about?

Five thousand hungry men, along with women and children, came to hear Jesus. But only one small boy had food—five loaves of bread and two fishes. The disciples didn't know what to do. But Jesus did! After He thanked God for the food, there was enough for all the people—plus some left over!

What's an important verse about the loaves and fishes?

Jesus. . .said to Philip, "Where can we buy bread to feed these people?" He said this to see what Philip would say. Jesus knew what He would do. Philip said to Him, "The money we have is not enough to buy bread to give each one a little."
JOHN 6:5–7 NLV

What does that mean to me?

Got a problem? Go to Jesus. He already knows the answer!

Lord of Peace

Who is the Lord of peace?

Jesus is!

What's it all about?

While Jesus was here on earth, He was blamed for something He didn't do. He was beaten and laughed at. He was whipped and then hung from a cross until He died. Through all this, He kept the peace of God.

What's an important verse about the Lord of peace?

Now may the Lord of peace himself give you his peace at all times and in every situation. The Lord be with you all.
2 Thessalonians 3:16 nlt

What does that mean to me?

Jesus knows everything you are going through—because He went through it all! He *Himself* will give you peace. He Himself walks with you—at all times and in every situation.

Manna from Heaven

What is manna from heaven?

Jesus—He is all we need!

What's it all about?

When the wandering Israelites were hungry in the wilderness, God rained down food from heaven. People had never seen it before, so they called it *manna*, which means, "What is it?"

What's an important verse about manna from heaven?

"Your ancestors ate manna in the wilderness, but they all died. Anyone who eats the bread from heaven, however, will never die. I am the living bread that came down from heaven."
JOHN 6:49–51 NLT

What does that mean to me?

If you are hungry, sad, angry, sorry, sick, in need, or feeling unloved, go to Jesus. He'll give you the one thing you need as you travel through life: nourishment from Him—forever and ever.

Martha

Who is Martha?

The sister of Mary and Lazarus of Bethany.

What's it all about?

Jesus made a visit to Martha and Mary's house. Martha was busy getting dinner ready. But Mary was doing nothing except sitting at Jesus' feet and listening to what He said. So Martha asked Jesus to make Mary help her.

What's an important verse about Martha?

"Martha, Martha," the Lord answered. "You are worried and upset about many things. . . . Only one thing is needed. Mary has chosen what is better. And it will not be taken away from her."
LUKE 10:41–42 NIrV

What does that mean to me?

Always make time to sit with Jesus. Just being with and listening to Him are the most important things you can do.

Mary of Bethany

Who is Mary of Bethany?

The sister of Martha and Lazarus.

What's it all about?

Mary loved listening to Jesus. After all, He was so wise and wonderful—He'd even saved her brother's life!

What's an important verse about Mary of Bethany?

Jesus came to Bethany, where Lazarus lived. Lazarus was the one Jesus had raised from the dead. . . . Then Mary took about a pint of pure nard. It was an expensive perfume. She poured it on Jesus' feet and wiped them with her hair. The house was filled with the sweet smell of the perfume.

JOHN 12:1, 3 NIrV

What does that mean to me?

Nothing is too good for Jesus. What special thing can *you* do for Him today?

Mary, the Mother of Jesus

Who is Mary, the mother of Jesus?

She is the virgin who gave birth to Jesus, the Son of God, and who married Joseph the carpenter.

What's it all about?

Mary was engaged to Joseph. The angel Gabriel told her she would get pregnant and become the mother of Jesus. Gabriel also told Mary that her cousin Elizabeth was pregnant—and that with God, anything is possible!

What's an important verse about Mary, the mother of Jesus?

Mary said to the angel, "How will this happen? I have never had a man." The angel said to her, "The Holy Spirit will come on you. . . . For God can do all things." Then Mary said, "I am willing to be used of the Lord. Let it happen to me as you have said." Then the angel went away from her.

LUKE 1:34–35, 37–38 NLV

What does that mean to me?

Believe God can do the impossible—through you. And He will!

Mary Magdalene

Who is Mary Magdalene?

A follower of Jesus and the first to see Him resurrected.

What's it all about?

After Jesus had chased seven demons out of Mary Magdalene, she followed Him everywhere. She watched Jesus being crucified and buried. But there was hope!

What's an important verse about Mary Magdalene?

Jesus said to her, "Mary! . . . Go to My brothers. Tell them that I will go up to My Father and your Father, and to My God and your God!" Mary Magdalene went and told the followers that she had seen the Lord.
JOHN 20:16–18 NLV

What does that mean to me?

Mary became a messenger to the messengers of the Good News. With whom can you share the hope of Jesus?

Matthew

Who is Matthew?

First he was a tax collector, then he became one of Jesus' main disciples. He wrote the Bible book of Matthew.

What's it all about?

In Jesus' day, tax collectors usually cheated people. And that's what Matthew did. Even so, Jesus told Matthew to follow Him. Then He had dinner with other sinners at Matthew's house.

What's an important verse about Matthew?

But when the Pharisees saw this, they asked his disciples, "Why does your teacher eat with such scum?" When Jesus heard this, he said. . . . "I have come to call not those who think they are righteous, but those who know they are sinners."
MATTHEW 9:11–13 NLT

What does that mean to me?

For Jesus, there is no lost cause when it comes to people. Who can you bring out the best in today?

Messiah

What is a messiah?

The word *messiah* means "the anointed one." In Greek, the word means "Christ." It's a term for a person who is set apart to serve God and is anointed with oil.

What's it all about?

In the Old Testament, prophets told the Jews that someone in David's family would forever rule God's people. So the Jews began looking for this forever messiah. Thousands of years later, the Messiah was born and called Jesus Christ.

What's an important verse about a messiah?

The woman said, "I know that Messiah is coming." Messiah means Christ. "When he comes, he will explain everything to us." Then Jesus said, "The one you're talking about is the one speaking to you. I am he."
JOHN 4:25–26 NIrV

What does that mean to me?

Are you ever confused? That's okay. Just go to Jesus. He's the King of all kings. He knows the answers to all your questions. He will show Himself to you and explain everything.

Miracle Worker

Who is the Miracle Worker?

Jesus is, was, and always will be!

What's it all about?

Jesus, the Son of God, had the power to heal people, chase demons, calm the wind, smooth out the sea, turn water into wine, raise the dead, and multiply loaves and fishes. Later, His followers did miracles, too—in Jesus' name!

What's an important verse about the Miracle Worker?

Jesus asked them, "Do you believe I can make you see?" "Yes, Lord," they told him, "we do." Then he touched their eyes and said, "Because of your faith, it will happen." Then their eyes were opened, and they could see!
MATTHEW 9:28–30 NLT

What does that mean to me?

If you have faith, Jesus can work a miracle in your life! Only believe!

Money Changers

Who are money changers?

Men who gave people Roman coins for Hebrew ones so that worshippers could buy an animal to sacrifice to God in the temple.

What's it all about?

Jesus believed that people should only be worshipping, praying, preaching, and learning about God in the temple—for it was *His* house, not a store where things could be bought and sold.

What's an important verse about money changers?

So Jesus. . .scattered the coins of the people exchanging money. And he turned over their tables. He told those who were selling doves, "Get these out of here! Stop turning my Father's house into a market!"
JOHN 2:15–16 NIrV

What does that mean to me?

When in church, focus on God—not money.

Nativity

What is the Nativity?

The birth of Jesus in Bethlehem. It's what we celebrate at Christmastime.

What's it all about?

Jesus, the one who would save the world, came in the form of a small, helpless baby born in a barn. Yet His coming was announced by an angel and a star led wise men to Him. They came and brought Him gifts. Shepherds also came to see the Lord of all.

What's an important verse about the Nativity?

While Joseph and Mary were there, the time came for the child to be born. She gave birth to her first baby. It was a boy. She wrapped him in large strips of cloth. Then she placed him in a manger. That's because there was no guest room where they could stay.

LUKE 2:6–7 NIrV

What does that mean to me?

Have you made room for Jesus in your heart? If not, why not make Him the star of your life today?

Nazareth

Where is Nazareth?

In Galilee.

What's it all about?

Nazareth is Jesus' hometown. That's why He was called Jesus of Nazareth.

What's an important verse about Nazareth?

Jesus left there and went to his hometown of Nazareth. His disciples went with him. . . . Jesus laid his hands on a few sick people and healed them. But he could not do any other miracles there. He was amazed because they had no faith.

MARK 6:1, 5–6 NIrV

What does that mean to me?

By not believing in Jesus, the people of Nazareth shut off His miracle-working power. Are you blocking Jesus' power in your life? Open up all of yourself to Him today and watch what He can do!

Nicodemus

Who is Nicodemus?

A Jewish ruler or Pharisee.

What's it all about?

Nicodemus was curious about Jesus, so he went to visit Him one night. Later, Nicodemus spoke up for Jesus when his fellow leaders wanted to arrest the Lord.

What's an important verse about Nicodemus?

Nicodemus went with Joseph. He was the man who had earlier visited Jesus at night. Nicodemus brought some mixed spices that weighed about 75 pounds. The two men took Jesus' body. They wrapped it in strips of linen cloth, along with the spices.

JOHN 19:39–40 NIrv

What does that mean to me?

The more you hang out with Jesus, the more you get to know Him and love Him. The more you know Him, the more you'll want to serve Him. Spend time with Jesus today. You'll be glad you did!

153 Fishes

What are the 153 fishes?

The number of fish Jesus' fishermen-followers caught.

What's it all about?

The followers of Jesus didn't know what to do after Jesus rose from the dead, so they went back to their jobs as fishermen. That night they didn't catch anything. The next morning, a stranger stood on the lakeshore. He told them where to cast their fishing net. They obeyed and caught 153 fish! *Then* they realized the stranger was Jesus.

What's an important verse about the 153 fishes?

Simon Peter went out and pulled the net to land. There were 153 big fish. The net was not broken even with so many. Jesus said to them, "Come and eat." Not one of the followers would ask, "Who are You?" They knew it was the Lord.

JOHN 21:11–12 NLV

What does that mean to me?

With Jesus nearby, you'll have success. Just do what He says!

Parables

What are parables?

Stories using ordinary things to teach extraordinary lessons.

What's it all about?

Jesus told lots of parables so that people could understand what He was trying to teach them.

What's an important verse about parables?

Jesus always used stories and illustrations like these when speaking to the crowds. In fact, he never spoke to them without using such parables. This fulfilled what God had spoken through the prophet: "I will speak to you in parables. I will explain things hidden since the creation of the world."

MATTHEW 13:34–35 NLT

What does that mean to me?

The more parables you understand, the more power you'll reveal in God's Word and the more secrets you'll know! What parable can you read—and share—today?

Paul (or Saul)

Who is Paul (or Saul)?

A Jewish leader named Saul who turned into a Christian named Paul.

What's it all about?

Saul was taking followers of Jesus to prison—or killing them! But one day God struck Saul blind and changed his heart—and life—forever.

What's an important verse about Paul (or Saul)?

Ananias. . .said, "Brother Saul, the Lord Jesus, who appeared to you on the road, has sent me so that you might regain your sight and be filled with the Holy Spirit." Instantly something like scales fell from Saul's eyes, and he regained his sight. Then he got up and was baptized. ACTS 9:17–18 NLT

What does that mean to me?

No matter what you've done, God can still use you!

Philip

Who is Philip?

A fisherman from Bethsaida and one of Jesus' main disciples.

What's it all about?

Right after he began following Jesus, Philip invited others to meet Him.

What's an important verse about Philip?

Philip went to look for Nathanael and told him, "We have found the very person Moses and the prophets wrote about! His name is Jesus, the son of Joseph from Nazareth." "Nazareth!" exclaimed Nathanael. "Can anything good come from Nazareth?" "Come and see for yourself," Philip replied.
JOHN 1:45–46 NLT

What does that mean to me?

Jesus wants many to be saved before He comes to visit us again. There's no time to lose! Who can you introduce Jesus to today?

Pontius Pilate

Who is Pontius Pilate?

A Roman governor of Judea.

What's it all about?

Jewish leaders wanted Pontius Pilate to crucify Jesus. Pilate's wife had a dream about Jesus and asked her husband not to kill Him. But even though Pilate knew Jesus was innocent, Pilate caved to the crowds and religious rulers.

What's an important verse about Pontius Pilate?

The people's shouts won out. So Pilate decided to give them what they wanted. . . . Pilate handed Jesus over to them so they could carry out their plans.
Luke 23:23–25 nirv

What does that mean to me?

Jesus wants you to stand up for what you believe in—even if you go against the crowd. So when it comes to choosing, choose Jesus—and you'll be on the right side every time.

Prayer

What is prayer?

Talking with God.

What's it all about?

God wants us to talk with Him! We can do that through prayer. Even if you don't know how to pray, God knows your heart. He'll understand what you are trying to say. And don't forget to pray in Jesus' name. Why? Check out this next verse!

What's an important verse about prayer?

"My Father will give you whatever you ask in My name. Until now you have not asked for anything in My name. Ask and you will receive. Then your joy will be full." JOHN 16:23–24 NLV

What does that mean to me?

Give your worries, thanks, joys, hopes, dreams, and blessings to God in prayer. Have faith that He has heard you. Then listen to what *He* has to say in return.

Preacher

What is a preacher?

Someone who gives people a message or sermon about God and the Good News of Jesus.

What's it all about?

Jesus preached in many places. He got many of His ideas across by telling parables, simple stories that ordinary people could understand.

What's an important verse about a preacher?

Preach the word. Be ready to serve God in good times and bad. Correct people's mistakes. Warn them. Encourage them with words of hope. Be very patient as you do these things. Teach them carefully.

2 TIMOTHY 4:2 NIrV

What does that mean to me?

One of the best ways to preach is to simply be a good example to others. Begin by following the Golden Rule. Then let your words *and* life "tell" other people about the Good News of Jesus.

Prodigal Son Parable

What is the Prodigal Son Parable?

A story Jesus told about a father and two sons.

What's it all about?

The younger son asked his dad for his half of the family money. Then this son went away and spent it all. He ended up so poor that he was not even able to afford *pig's* food. So he decided to go home, tell his dad he made a mistake, and ask him for a job. The dad not only welcomed his son back home but also celebrated his return!

"While the son was still a long way off, his father saw him. He was filled with tender love for his son. He ran to him. He threw his arms around him and kissed him."
LUKE 15:20 NIrV

What does that mean to me?

If you feel lost, go to God. He welcomes all who come home to Him with arms wide open.

Resurrection

What is the Resurrection?

When Jesus rose up from the grave three days after He died on the cross.

What's it all about?

After His friend Lazarus died, Jesus resurrected him—He brought Lazarus back from the dead. After Jesus died, His body was taken down from the cross and put in a tomb that was closed up by a big rock. Three days later, the stone was rolled away, and God's power raised Jesus from the dead. Many people saw Jesus alive. That is *the* Resurrection!

What's an important verse about the Resurrection?

Jesus told her, "I am the resurrection and the life. Anyone who believes in me will live, even after dying."
JOHN 11:25 NLT

What does that mean to me?

Without Jesus in our lives, our spirits are dead. Believe in Him today, and your spirit will live forever!

Road to Emmaus

What is the road to Emmaus?

The seven-mile road leading from Jerusalem to Emmaus, about a two-hour walk.

What's it all about?

Two of Jesus' followers were walking to Emmaus three days after Jesus had died. A stranger joined them. He asked why they were so sad. So they told him everything that had happened to Jesus and invited the stranger to dinner. Then something amazing happened. . . .

What's an important verse about the road to Emmaus?

The two from Emmaus told their story of how Jesus had appeared to them as they were walking along the road, and how they had recognized him as he was breaking the bread. And just as they were telling about it, Jesus himself was suddenly standing there among them. "Peace be with you," he said.

LUKE 24:35–36 NLT

What does that mean to me?

Whenever and wherever Jesus shows up, peace and joy follow!

Rock

Who is the Rock?

Jesus. He protects and strengthens us.

What's it all about?

Jesus is the Rock we can build our lives on. He is our spiritual Rock. Nothing—and no one—can topple Him!

What's an important verse about the Rock?

"So then, everyone who hears my words and puts them into practice is like a wise man. He builds his house on the rock. The rain comes down. The water rises. The winds blow and beat against that house. But it does not fall. It is built on the rock."
MATTHEW 7:24–25 NIrV

What does that mean to me?

Don't just listen to the Word—live it! Stand on it! And you'll be rock solid!

Savior

Who is the Savior?

Jesus Christ is—He rescued us!

What's it all about?

People couldn't obey all the laws of Moses. We kept sinning, or "missing the mark," which kept us separated from God. So God sent Jesus to earth, and Jesus sacrificed (gave up) His life to save ours.

What's an important verse about the Savior?

For God saved us and called us to live a holy life. . . . He has made all of this plain to us by the appearing of Christ Jesus, our Savior. He broke the power of death and illuminated the way to life and immortality through the Good News.

2 TIMOTHY 1:9–10 NLT

What does that mean to me?

Believe in Jesus, and He will be your Savior forever and ever!

Second Coming

What is the Second Coming?

When Jesus returns for the last time.

What's it all about?

Jesus will come back again. When He does, believers—living and dead—will rise up and join Him forever and ever in heaven.

What's an important verse about the Second Coming?

Christ was offered up once. He took away the sins of many people. He will also come a second time. At that time he will not suffer for sin. Instead, he will come to bring salvation to those who are waiting for him.
HEBREWS 9:28 NIrV

What does that mean to me?

You can always trust Jesus. He's someone worth waiting for—whether in heaven or on earth.

Sermon on the Mount

What is the Sermon on the Mount?

A message Jesus gave while standing on a hill. You can read His full sermon in Matthew 5–7.

What's it all about?

The Sermon on the Mount tells people how they should live for God. It's not just about doing a certain thing (on the outside), but also being a certain way (on the inside). Only someone who truly believes in Jesus can live according to the Sermon on the Mount.

What's an important verse about the Sermon on the Mount?

Jesus went up on the mountainside and sat down. His disciples gathered around him, and he began to teach them.
MATTHEW 5:1–2 NLT

What does that mean to me?

Do you believe in Jesus—from the inside out?

Simon of Cyrene

Who is Simon of Cyrene?

The man who helped Jesus carry His cross to Golgotha.

What's it all about?

Jesus had been beaten, whipped, and laughed at. Then He was made to carry His heavy wooden cross to the place where He would be crucified. At some point, Jesus needed help.

What's an important verse about Simon of Cyrene?

A man named Simon, who was from Cyrene, happened to be coming in from the countryside. The soldiers seized him and put the cross on him and made him carry it behind Jesus.
LUKE 23:26 NLT

What does that mean to me?

We must carry our own cross to follow Jesus. That means working with and for Him as His servants. Who can you help along the way?

Simon Peter

Who is Simon Peter?

A brother to Andrew, a fisherman, and one of Jesus' main disciples. His name means "rock."

What's it all about?

Peter really loved Jesus. Even though he made lots of mistakes—like sinking in the sea for lack of faith and later denying he even *knew* Jesus—Jesus used Peter to build up the Church.

What's an important verse about Simon Peter?

Those who believed what Peter said were baptized and added to the church that day—about 3,000 in all.
ACTS 2:41 NLT

What does that mean to me?

If you make a mistake, don't fret. Go to Jesus. Ask for His help in making things right, and He'll use you to lead others to Him.

Son of David

Who is the Son of David?

Jesus—our prophet, priest, and king! Through His mother, Mary, Jesus is an heir of David by blood. Through His foster father, Joseph, Jesus is in line for King David's throne!

What's it all about?

Many years ago, God promised King David's throne and kingdom would last forever. So Jews knew that the one who would save them (the Messiah) would be from David's family.

What's an important verse about the Son of David?

This is the written story of the family line of Jesus the Messiah. He is the son of David.
MATTHEW 1:1 NIrV

What does that mean to me?

Don't worry about anything. God is in control and keeps His promises and plans. Just obey King Jesus, and all will be well!

Son of God

Who is the Son of God?

Jesus—our friend and king!

What's it all about?

Jesus was conceived in Mary by the Holy Spirit. That makes Him God's Son. And Jesus is just like His Father God!

What's an important verse about the Son of God?

As soon as Jesus was baptized. . .heaven was opened. Jesus saw the Spirit of God coming down on him like a dove. A voice from heaven said, "This is my Son, and I love him. I am very pleased with him."
MATTHEW 3:16–17 NIrV

What does that mean to me?

When you believe in Jesus, you become one of God's children—which makes you Jesus' brother or sister! Welcome to an amazing family!

Son of Man

Who is the Son of Man?

Jesus—our brother and lord!

What's it all about?

Jesus told His followers He was the Son of Man, or Messiah, the prophet Daniel saw many years ago. As the Son of Man, Jesus was one of us—even though He was also God. Being part human, Jesus felt everything we feel.

What's an important verse about the Son of Man?

Jesus replied, "Foxes have dens. Birds have nests. But the Son of Man has no place to lay his head."
LUKE 9:58 NIrV

What does that mean to me?

Jesus wants a home in you. Make room for Him in your heart, and feel free to tell Him everything you feel. He understands!

Spirit of Christ

What is the Spirit of Christ?

Having the Spirit of God living in you, making you like Jesus.

What's it all about?

When you let Jesus into your heart, the Holy Spirit comes inside you. He helps guide you to where God wants you to go by molding you to be like Jesus Christ.

What's an important verse about the Spirit of Christ?

But you are not ruled by the power of sin. Instead, the Holy Spirit rules over you. This is true if the Spirit of God lives in you. Anyone who does not have the Spirit of Christ does not belong to Christ.
ROMANS 8:9 NIrv

What does that mean to me?

Follow in Jesus' footsteps, and you will never be lost.

Teacher

What is a teacher?

Someone who helps you to learn.

What's it all about?

Many people—both friends and enemies—called Jesus "teacher." He told lots of parables. Some listened only to try to trick Him; others just wanted to learn more about God.

What's an important verse about a teacher?

"And don't address anyone here on earth as 'Father,' for only God in heaven is your spiritual Father. And don't let anyone call you 'Teacher,' for you have only one teacher, the Messiah."
MATTHEW 23:9–10 NLT

What does that mean to me?

Jesus is the greatest of your teachers. Make sure that His lessons are the main ones you learn.

Temple Dedication

What is temple dedication?

When a baby was dedicated (committed) to God in the Jerusalem Temple.

What's it all about?

Jewish law said that babies were to be presented to God in the temple when they were eight days old. So Joseph and Mary took Jesus there, along with two birds to sacrifice. Two people at the temple—Simeon and Anna—knew Jesus was someone special right away, that He had been sent by God to rescue His people.

What's an important verse about temple dedication?

Jesus' parents were amazed at what was being said about him.

LUKE 2:33 NLT

What does that mean to me?

You know Jesus is special, too! Is what you are saying about Him amazing others?

Temptation

What is temptation?

When someone or something urges you to do something you shouldn't do.

What is it all about?

After His baptism, the Spirit led Jesus into the wilderness. For forty days He ate nothing and was tempted three times by the devil. The devil tried to get Jesus to:

- doubt His Father God's care,
- accept the world and worship him (the devil) alone, and
- test God's protection.

With each temptation, Jesus defeated the devil by quoting a verse from the Bible.

What is an important verse about temptation?

Jesus said to the devil, "Get behind Me, Satan! For it is written, 'You must worship the Lord your God. You must obey Him only.'"
LUKE 4:8 NLV

Get to know your Bible. Then you, too, can beat the devil and put him behind you!

Thomas

Who is Thomas?

One of Jesus' main disciples, who was also called the Twin.

What's it all about?

After Jesus rose from the dead, He appeared to His disciples—but Thomas wasn't there. When the others told Thomas that the Lord had appeared to them, Thomas didn't believe them. So the Lord came again eight days later. Then Thomas *did* believe!

What's an important verse about Thomas?

"Don't be faithless any longer. Believe!"... Then Jesus told him, "You believe because you have seen me. Blessed are those who believe without seeing me."
JOHN 20:27, 29 NLT

What does that mean to me?

How wonderful that you believe in Jesus—even though you haven't seen Him! That makes you an extra-special believer to Jesus.

Tomb

What is a tomb?

A place where people were buried.

What's it all about?

Joseph of Arimathea had a tomb carved out of rock. After laying Jesus' dead body in the tomb, Joseph rolled a big stone in front of it so that no one could get in. But when women went to visit the grave three days later, the stone had been rolled away!

What's an important verse about a tomb?

The angel said, "Don't be alarmed. You are looking for Jesus of Nazareth, who was crucified. He isn't here! He is risen from the dead!"
MARK 16:6 NLT

What does that mean to me?

Jesus Christ is alive—and always will be. That's something to cheer about, for nothing can hold Him down—not even death!

Transfiguration

What is the Transfiguration?

When Jesus was so transformed that His face was as bright as the sun and His clothes were as white as light.

What's it all about?

Jesus took His followers Peter, James, and John to a mountaintop. His appearance was transfigured. Just then Moses and Elijah appeared and began talking with Jesus. A cloud came down from heaven and surrounded them all.

What's an important verse about the Transfiguration?

A bright cloud covered them. A voice from the cloud said, "This is my Son, and I love him. I am very pleased with him. Listen to him!"
MATTHEW 17:5 NIrV

What does that mean to me?

If you listen to Jesus, you, too, will be transformed—and that'll please God!

The Trinity

What is the Trinity?

God is three persons in one: the Father, Jesus the Son, and the Holy Spirit.

What's it all about?

God's power helps us stick close to Jesus. Jesus shows us how to live. The Holy Spirit is God's pledge that we will receive all He promised.

What's an important verse about the Trinity?

God is the One Who makes our faith and your faith strong in Christ. He has set us apart for Himself. He has put His mark on us to show we belong to Him. His Spirit is in our hearts to prove this.

2 CORINTHIANS 1:21–22 NLV

What does that mean to me?

If you're a believer, God, Jesus, and the Spirit are all on your side—inside and out!

Triumphal Entry

What is the Triumphal Entry?

When Jesus rode a donkey into Jerusalem, five days before going to the cross. We know and celebrate it today as Palm Sunday.

What's it all about?

Prophets long ago had predicted Jesus' Triumphal Entry. In all four Gospels, you can read the story about how people cheered Him and threw palm branches on the road in front of Him.

What's an important verse about the Triumphal Entry?

Jesus found a young donkey and sat on it. The Holy Writings say, "Do not be afraid, people of Jerusalem. See! Your King comes sitting on a young donkey!"
JOHN 12:14–15 NLV

What does that mean to me?

Your humble Savior and King is not gone—so do not fear, but cheer! He lives forever in heaven—and in your heart!

Two Thieves

Who are the two thieves?

Criminals crucified with Jesus, one on each side.

What's it all about?

The first thief made fun of Jesus, but the second thief yelled at the first for mocking God. The second thief knew that he and the other thief were guilty of their crimes and that Jesus was not. He knew he had no hope—except for Jesus.

What's an important verse about the two thieves?

He said to Jesus, "Lord, remember me when You come into Your holy nation." Jesus said to him, "For sure, I tell you, today you will be with Me in Paradise."
LUKE 23:42–43 NLV

What does that mean to me?

Jesus suffered to bring all to Paradise who are true of heart and believe in Him. Do you believe?

Vine

Who is the Vine?

Jesus! And God is the gardener.

What's it all about?

Jesus, the Word made flesh, is the true Vine. He has been planted in the earth. From Him, we believers, the branches, get all our support, food, and water. With Jesus holding us up and feeding us, we can bear fruit!

What's an important verse about the Vine?

"No branch can give fruit by itself. It has to get life from

the vine. You are able to give fruit only when you have life from Me. I am the Vine and you are the branches. Get your life from Me. Then I will live in you and you will give much fruit. You can do nothing without Me."
JOHN 15:4–5 NLV

What does that mean to me?

If you stick close to Jesus and keep His Word in your heart, you'll be able to do what He calls you to do, *and* you'll bring glory to God!

Walks on Water

Who walks on water?

Jesus—and Peter, for a moment or two!

What's it all about?

Jesus' followers were rowing their boat. Then the wind picked up, and the waves started to grow bigger. Next thing His followers knew, they saw Jesus walking toward their boat. Peter started walking on the water but then took his eyes off Jesus.

What's an important verse about walking on water?

Peter called to him, "Lord, if it's really you, tell me to come to you, walking on the water." "Yes, come," Jesus said. So Peter went over the side of the boat and walked on the water toward Jesus. But when he saw the strong wind and the waves, he was terrified and began to sink. "Save me, Lord!" he shouted. Jesus immediately reached out and grabbed him.

MATTHEW 14:28–31 NLT

What does that mean to me?

Never fear. Jesus is near. Just keep your eyes on Him. He will save you!

Way, Truth, and Life

Who is the Way, the Truth, and the Life?

Jesus is!

What's it all about?

Jesus is the Way; in Him, God and man are brought together. He is the Truth; He is right and honest. He is the Life; for our spirits only come alive through Christ in God.

What's an important verse about the Way, the Truth, and the Life?

Thomas said to Jesus, "Lord, we do not know where You are going. How can we know the way to get there?" Jesus said, "I am the Way and the Truth and the Life. No one can go to the Father except by Me."
JOHN 14:5–6 NLV

What does that mean to me?

Jesus is all you ever need, so make your *way* through *life* in *truth* with Him!

Wise Men

Who are the wise men?

Really smart men who followed a star.

What's it all about?

Wise men were looking for the King of the Jews. So King Herod told them to let him know when they found Him, because Herod wanted to kill Him.

What's an important verse about the wise men?

The Wise Men. . .saw the child with his mother Mary. They bowed down and worshiped him. Then they opened their treasures. They gave him gold, frankincense and myrrh. But God warned them in a dream not to go back to Herod. So they returned to their country on a different road.

MATTHEW 2:11–12 NIrV

What does that mean to me?

No one can outsmart God. Follow Him and His Word, and you'll be wise, too!

Woman Who Bled

Who is the woman who bled?

A woman who had been bleeding for 12 years.

What's it all about?

No doctors could cure her, so this woman looked for Jesus, found Him, and reached for His robe. She was *sure* He could heal her. As soon as she touched Him, she stopped bleeding!

What's an important verse about the woman who bled?

Jesus knew that power had gone from Him. . . . He said to her, "Daughter, your faith has healed you. Go in peace and be free from your sickness."
MARK 5:30, 34 NLV

What does that mean to me?

When you have faith in Jesus and reach out for Him, His power will make amazing things happen. Reach out today!

The Word

Who is the Word?

Jesus is!

What's it all about?

Jesus has been around since the beginning of time. He was with God when He spoke, creating the earth and heavens. And then the Word (Jesus Christ) became human and lived on earth. He—the Word—tells us what God wants us to know.

What's an important verse about the Word?

The Word (Christ) was in the beginning. The Word was with God. The Word was God. He was with God in the beginning. . . . Christ became human flesh and lived among us.
JOHN 1:1–2, 14 NLV

What does that mean to me?

Jesus always was, is, and will be here for you. That's a good word you can hold in your heart forever and ever.

Zion

What is Zion?

Another name for Jerusalem, parts of Jerusalem, its people, and the eternal city of God.

What's it all about?

Jesus is
- the King the prophets said would come into the City of Zion, riding on a donkey,
- the Lamb who would stand on Mount Zion, and
- the Stone in Zion.

What's an important verse about Zion?

In Scripture it says, "Look! I am placing a stone in Zion. It is a chosen and very valuable stone. It is the most important stone in the building. The one who trusts in him will never be put to shame."
1 PETER 2:6 NIrV

What does that mean to me?

Be proud of the strength of Jesus. When you make Him the most important thing in your life, your Cornerstone, the love of God will shine through and in you—whether you are on earth or in heaven!

Check out other
KNOW YOUR BIBLE FOR KIDS
titles

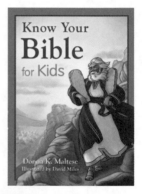